SCIENCE FIGHTS BACK

SCIENCE
Vs
NATURAL DISASTERS

by Angela Royston

raintree
a Capstone company — publishers for children

Raintree is an imprint of Capstone Global Library Limited, a company incorporated in England and Wales having its registered office at 264 Banbury Road, Oxford OX2 7DY – Registered company number: 6695582

www.raintree.co.uk
myorders@raintree.co.uk

Text © Capstone Global Library Limited 2016
The moral rights of the proprietor have been asserted.

Produced for Raintree by Calcium
Edited by Sarah Eason and Amanda Learmonth
Designed by Simon Borrough
Picture research by Rachel Blount
Production by Victoria Fitzgerald
Originated by Capstone Global Library © 2016
Printed and bound in China

ISBN 978 1 4747 1616 1
19 18 17 16 15
10 9 8 7 6 5 4 3 2 1

British Library Cataloguing in Publication Data
A full catalogue record for this book is available from the British Library.

Acknowledgements
We would like to thank the following for permission to reproduce photographs: Dreamstime: Aberration 29, Ackleyroadphotos 26, Adpower99 31, Anharris 27, Aurinko 20b, Cryssfotos 4, Curioustiger 25, Darkdante 7, Digitalfestival 38, Emiliau 36, Hansenn 35, Irfannurd 33, Jianbinglee 28, 45b, Kated 13, Mike Kiev 16, Lightningtodd 18, 44br, Marbo 40, Marekpilar 5, 44t, MinervaStudio 19, Moth 39, Mtrommer 16–17, 45tl, Myersct 37, Olesiaru 9, Morgan Oliver 22, 45c, Pancaketom 20–21, 44bl, Pashapixel 24, Robybret 42, Rudmary5 43, Sergehorta 34, Soleilc 8, Staphy 14, 15, Typhoonski 32, Visdia 10, Wildmac 12, Wongsrikul 41t; Shutterstock: Arindambanerjee 43tr, Pavel Dudek 30, Dutourdumonde Photography 11, EcoPrint 23, Somjin Klong-ugkara 6.

Cover photographs reproduced with permission of: Dreamstime: Martin Haas (br); Shutterstock: M.D. (tl).

Every effort has been made to contact copyright holders of material reproduced in this book. Any omissions will be rectified in subsequent printings if notice is given to the publisher.

All the internet addresses (URLs) given in this book were valid at the time of going to press. However, due to the dynamic nature of the internet, some addresses may have changed, or sites may have changed or ceased to exist since publication. While the author and publisher regret any inconvenience this may cause readers, no responsibility for any such changes can be accepted by either the author or the publisher.

Some words are shown in bold, **like this**. You can find out what they mean by looking in the glossary.

Contents

Disasters of nature

Natural disasters have been part of Earth's history since before life began. Volcanic eruptions, earthquakes, huge storms, floods, giant waves and **droughts** have all helped to form our planet. Our ancestors did not understand why these terrifying events happened or when they might strike next. They feared them even more than we do.

Dreaded waves
A **tsunami** wave is a horrific sight for people who live in tsunami danger zones.

NATURAL FORCES

Natural disasters unleash powerful forces. Earthquakes under the ocean cause tsunamis, with huge waves that can flood the coast and sweep inland. Anyone in the way is likely to be killed. Earthquakes and volcanoes are **seismic** events that shake the ground or the ocean floor. Red-hot **lava** and clouds of ash erupt from volcanoes.

DEADLY STORMS

Hurricanes and **tornadoes** bring heavy rain and devastating winds. A tornado's whirling winds are so powerful they can lift trucks into the air and flatten houses. Hurricanes cause huge waves that combine with high tides and result in **storm surges** that flood the coast. Floods from storm surges and rain can turn motorways into rivers and wash away cars and even buildings.

BLIZZARD CHAOS

Blizzards cause havoc, and they can go on for months. Snow blocks motorways and airports, cutting off towns and villages. Droughts can last for many months or even years, turning large areas into desert.

THE FIGHT BACK

Scientists now have a greater understanding of what causes earthquakes, hurricanes and other natural disasters. They cannot prevent them occurring, but they are getting better at predicting when they are likely to take place. They are also looking for ways to protect people from some of the dangers.

Winning or losing?

Many people think that extreme weather is becoming more common and even getting worse. Scientists record and measure disasters to find out what is happening. They also look at underlying causes, such as the temperature of the air and the oceans, to understand why disasters might be getting worse.

Crash of thunder
Lightning accompanies thunderstorms, which often cause heavy rain and flooding.

Chapter one: The battleground

Natural disasters cause catastrophic damage. They can kill and injure hundreds of thousands of people. They devastate crops and kill farm animals. Natural disasters can destroy villages, towns and cities, too. The battleground for extreme weather begins in the sky, but for seismic events it begins deep below the ground.

RECENT DISASTERS

Many natural disasters have occurred in recent years. In April 2015, an earthquake in Nepal, southern Asia, killed over 8,000 people. The earthquake triggered an **avalanche** on the world's highest mountain, Mount Everest, killing several mountain climbers. In 2014, a **cyclone** struck the east coast of India, bringing strong winds that damaged thousands of people's homes and their crops. In 2011, a huge tsunami hit the northeast of Japan. Waves up to 40.5 metres (133 feet) surged 10 kilometres (6 miles) inland, much further than any tsunami had before.

Country in ruins
The earthquake that struck the Asian country of Nepal in 2015 destroyed many of its towns and villages.

UNPREDICTABLE WEATHER

The weather around the world is becoming more unpredictable, making it harder for people to deal with. If a region usually floods at a particular time of the year, people can learn to prepare for that. In Southern Asia, for example, **monsoon** winds bring rain and floods between October and December. People rely on the monsoon rains to water their crops and farmland.

CLIMATE CHANGE

Many people are now asking why the weather is more unpredictable and why extreme weather is becoming worse. Many scientists think it is because of **global warming** – an increase in the average temperature on Earth's surface. Global warming coincides with humans burning more **fossil fuels** – oil, coal and natural gas. Climates around the world are changing, and even worse natural disasters could still be to come.

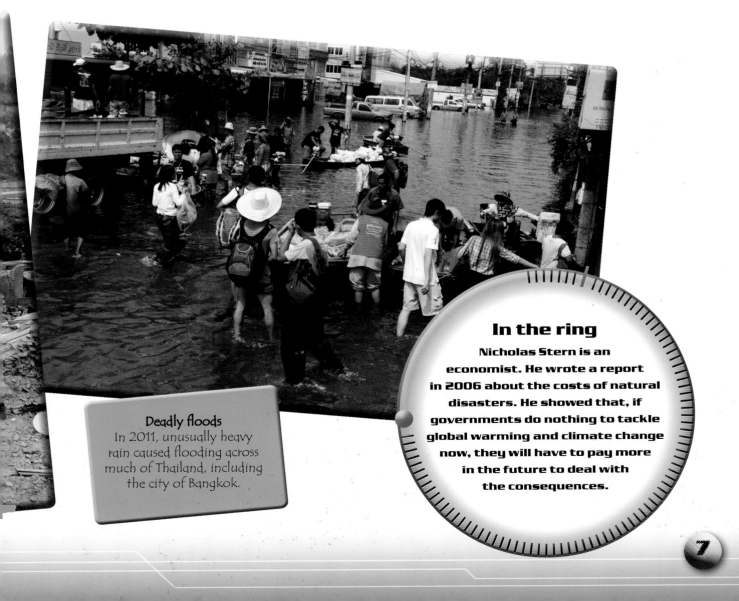

Deadly floods
In 2011, unusually heavy rain caused flooding across much of Thailand, including the city of Bangkok.

In the ring

Nicholas Stern is an economist. He wrote a report in 2006 about the costs of natural disasters. He showed that, if governments do nothing to tackle global warming and climate change now, they will have to pay more in the future to deal with the consequences.

What causes the weather?

The weather is what happens in the layer of air that is closest to Earth's surface. The air, or atmosphere, consists mainly of the gases nitrogen and oxygen. It also contains water vapour, carbon dioxide and other gases. The weather is driven by the heat of the Sun.

Unexpected snowfall
Weather is becoming not just unpredictable, but bizarre. This snow fell in a desert that is normally hot and dry.

WHAT MAKES WEATHER

The main elements of the weather are the temperature of the air, wind and rain. The Sun is behind all of three of these. As the Sun's heat warms water in the ocean and on land, some of it evaporates, forming water vapour in the air. It falls back to Earth as rain, snow, hail or sleet. The Sun heats some parts of the atmosphere more than others. The warmer air in these areas rises, pulling in cooler air to replace it. The moving air is wind.

TRAPPING HEAT

Clouds trap some of the Sun's heat and stop it from escaping back into space. Carbon dioxide, methane and other gases also trap heat. Burning fossil fuels releases carbon dioxide. It is these gases that cause global warming. Some of the heat that reaches the oceans and the ground is reflected straight back into space, but some of the heat is absorbed. White surfaces, such as snow and ice, reflect more heat than dark surfaces, such as seawater. The more heat that remains trapped, the higher the average temperature of Earth's surface.

Patches on the Sun
The dark patches on the surface of the Sun are the sunspots. The spots look small, but each one is larger than Earth.

Understanding earthquakes and tsunamis

The ground beneath our feet may feel firm, but it is just a crust of solid rock that floats on a mass of molten rock called **magma**. Earth's crust is divided into huge plates which carry the continents and the ocean floor on top of them. The plates are pushed slowly by **currents** in the magma.

Cracked Earth
The fiery red lines on this model of Earth show the edges of its plates. It is here that most volcanoes and earthquakes occur.

HOW PLATES MOVE

Some plates are moving apart, some are moving towards each other and other plates slowly slide past each other. The trouble occurs when two plates become jammed, or the pressure between them builds up. The plates then suddenly move with a jerk, which releases a vast amount of energy. The energy shakes the ground and can create cracks in it. If the earthquake is under the ocean, the sudden movement of one plate over another disturbs the water and creates a tsunami.

AFTERSHOCKS

An earthquake is not just one event. Small **earth tremors** usually occur first. If the tremors become bigger, it is a sign that a major earthquake could follow. Aftershocks are earthquakes that come after the main quake and happen as the plates continue to move. Aftershocks can continue for days, weeks or even months. Buildings that have been weakened by the main quake may collapse in an aftershock.

In the ring

Alfred Wegener (1880–1930) put forward the theory of moving plates in 1915. Like many people, he had noticed that the shapes of the continents fit together like the pieces of a giant jigsaw. He realized that at one time the continents had indeed been joined together in one huge continent. They had slowly changed their position over hundreds of millions of years. He called this continental drift.

Destroyed buildings

In May 2015, a few weeks after the devastating earthquake hit Nepal, a powerful aftershock in the city of Kathmandu caused more buildings to collapse.

11

What causes a volcano to erupt?

A volcano forms where there is a crack or weak place in Earth's crust. Magma pushes through the crust and spills out, along with gases and sometimes ash. Once the red-hot liquid rock has reached the surface, it is called lava. It pours down the side of the volcano and cools to form solid black rock. The lava adds another layer of rock to the mountain, making it bigger and taller.

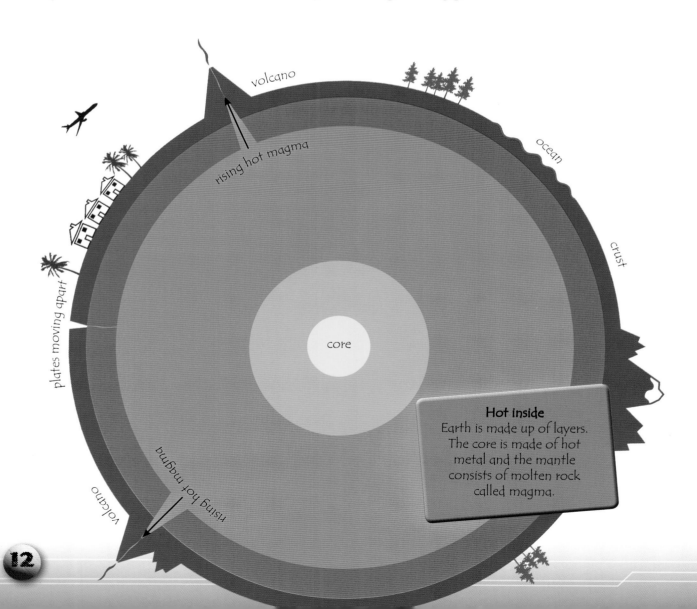

volcano

rising hot magma

ocean

crust

plates moving apart

core

rising hot magma

volcano

Hot inside
Earth is made up of layers. The core is made of hot metal and the mantle consists of molten rock called magma.

INSIDE A VOLCANO

A volcanic eruption begins in the magma chamber, deep inside the volcano. The level of magma in the chamber varies. Sometimes there is so much magma that it is pushed out of the chamber and into the volcano's **vents**. The main vent leads to a cone at the top of the mountain, and side vents inside the volcano open onto its side.

TYPES OF ERUPTION

How a volcano erupts depends on how runny the magma is and how much gas it contains. When the magma is thick and contains a lot of gas, the volcano will suddenly explode. Explosive volcanoes blast hot gases and ash high into the air. They also cause landslides and mudslides. Explosive volcanoes are the most dangerous volcanoes. Volcanoes that have runny magma with less gas erupt gently almost all the time. They are called effusive volcanoes, and they are much less destructive.

Winning or losing?

Volcanoes can be destructive, but they have positive benefits, too. The soil on the slopes of volcanoes is **fertile** and is good for growing crops. That is why so many people live close to volcanoes. Geysers are volcanoes that spew hot water instead of lava. In Iceland, for example, geysers provide free hot water and warm swimming pools all year. They are also used to generate electricity. Some underwater volcanoes grow tall enough to form islands, such as the Hawaiian islands.

Preserved in ash

When Mount Vesuvius in Italy erupted in AD 79, the victims of the disaster were preserved in volcanic ash.

Chapter two: Watching the weather

Predicting the weather is the first stage in dealing with natural weather disasters. If you know that extreme weather is coming, you can prepare for it. This is the job of special scientists called **meteorologists**. They gather weather information from around the world and work out what might happen next in particular places, or with certain storms and weather systems.

COLLECTING INFORMATION

Meteorologists use many different methods to collect data. Weather stations have instruments that measure different aspects of the weather. Anemometers, for example, measure the speed and direction of the wind. Rain gauges collect and measure the amount of rain that has fallen. Other instruments measure the amount of water vapour in the air and the temperature and the pressure of the air. Most importantly, the instruments record how these measurements are changing. Weather balloons record what is happening higher in the atmosphere.

Into the atmosphere
A weather balloon lifts a meteorological probe high into the sky to gather data in the atmosphere.

COMPUTER MODELS

In space, satellites take photographs of the clouds and surface of Earth. They give meteorologists a picture of what is happening over a large area. Meteorologists study the information and put it into computers. The computers help them to predict what will happen next. Meteorologists can make accurate predictions for a day or two ahead. However, the weather is so complicated it is much harder to make accurate long-term weather forecasts.

Icy landscape
Antarctica is a continent covered by ice. The ice is up to several kilometres deep in some places.

Breaking through

Meteorologists study weather in the past as well as in the present. Scientists use a hollow drill to remove a large tube, or core, of ice from the Arctic or Antarctic. An ice core that was taken recently from Antarctica has allowed scientists to study ice that is more than 800,000 years old. So far, every ice core has shown that the temperature of Earth increased at points in time when the amount of carbon dioxide in the air also increased.

Predicting and tracking storms

A hurricane begins as a storm over the oceans in the tropics. The spin of the Earth causes the winds to whirl around the centre of the storm. The storm moves across the oceans, sometimes gaining and sometimes losing strength. It may die out while it is still over the ocean, or it may move over islands or reach the mainland. As it moves over land, it weakens and dies out.

Bending with the wind
Palm trees are battered in hurricane winds, but the trees' trunks are **flexible** so they bend, rather than snap.

View from space
This photograph of a hurricane was taken by a satellite in space.

HOW A HURRICANE FORMS

A tropical storm is fed by hot, damp air that rises from the warm ocean water. As the hot air rises, it pulls in cooler winds. The faster the hot air rises, the stronger are the winds that are pulled in around it. The storm becomes a hurricane when the wind is over 119 kilometres per hour (74 mph). A hurricane can be hundreds of kilometres wide. The winds become stronger the closer they are to the centre of the storm. The centre itself is called the eye and, amazingly, it is calm with little or no wind. Around the eye are thick clouds carrying heavy rain and thunderstorms.

TRACKING A STORM

Meteorologists use satellite photos to track how a storm is developing and the path it is taking. They plot the position of the eye every six hours. Aeroplanes called Hurricane Hunters fly right into the centre of the hurricane. They measure the conditions in the atmosphere, and their readings give the meteorologists information about what is happening inside the storm.

Winning or losing?

It is very difficult to predict the path and strength of a storm. A hurricane can suddenly change direction and head off on a new path. It changes strength when it passes over a warmer or cooler area of ocean. Meteorologists have studied many storms, but they can never be sure exactly what will happen next. They issue warnings telling people what they think is most likely to happen.

Predicting tornadoes

A tornado is a smaller but more powerful storm than a hurricane. Tornadoes only travel over land, but hurricanes begin at sea and then hit the coast and move inland. A tornado may measure less than 91 metres (100 yards) across and last for only a few minutes. Its winds are stronger than those in a hurricane, and they spin tightly around the centre. The tornado sucks up all kinds of debris, from dust and rubbish to whole trees and even cars. As the tornado loses strength, these objects drop back down to the ground.

Terrible twister
Tornadoes can carry hailstones in their clouds, which batter the ground below the funnel.

In the ring

Most people want to avoid tornadoes, but storm chasers try their best to find them! They get as close as possible to tornadoes to study them as they happen. Storm chasers drive trucks equipped with cameras, radar, radio and meteorological instruments. They keep in contact with the weather centre to get the latest updates on thunderstorms that might produce tornadoes. Many storm chasers are meteorologists, but others are people who just enjoy the thrill of a severe storm.

HOW A TORNADO FORMS

Most tornadoes form beneath thunderclouds, particularly those that have strong updraughts. These are winds that blow upwards. When the wind begins to spin, a tornado is born. A funnel of spinning, rising wind forms under the cloud. The funnel grows longer until it reaches the ground. As the tornado loses strength, the funnel becomes weaker and shrinks back into the cloud.

The aftermath

Tornadoes can cause devastation, overturning vehicles and stripping the leaves and bark off trees.

LOOKING FOR TORNADOES

The place where tornadoes are most common is an area of the Great Plains in the United States. It has so many tornadoes that it is called "Tornado Alley". Each tornado lasts only for a short time, but one tornado after another can form under very violent thunderstorms. Tornadoes are very hard to predict. Meteorologists can predict the path of severe storms, but not exactly when or where a tornado may form.

Warning the public

The second weapon in the scientists' fight against extreme weather is warning the public. If people know what is coming, they can protect themselves and their property. In the United States, meteorologists issue two levels of warning. A hurricane, tornado or flood watch means any of these disasters are possible. A warning means a hurricane, tornado or flood is likely to occur.

DISASTER WATCH

People who live in areas that are often hit by hurricanes, tornadoes or floods plan what they will do in the event of a disaster. People decide where to go if they have to evacuate their homes and check the route they will take to get there. When a watch is issued, people stock up with food, medicines and other essentials. They fill their cars with petrol, and check that they have torches and other equipment in case the electricity is cut off.

Personal warning
People can now receive warnings on their smartphones that a tornado is heading their way.

20

Unexpected warning
Even deserts can suffer from floods. This sign in Utah, United States, warns of flash floods, which strike after heavy rain.

DISASTER WARNING

When a warning is issued, people prepare for the disaster by protecting their homes. They bring outdoor furniture, toys and loose items inside. If a hurricane or tornado is likely, they can protect their homes by boarding up windows and securing doors. If a flood is expected, they may move carpets and electrical devices, such as televisions, computers and games consoles, as high above the ground as they can, usually upstairs.

Breaking through

It is important that meteorologists get their warnings right. If there are many false alarms, people begin to ignore them. Tornadoes are so hard to predict accurately that many people do not take the warnings seriously. Weather services in countries such as the United States, Japan and Canada now send out automatic warnings directly to people's mobile phones to alert them if a natural disaster is about to occur in their area.

Long-term forecasts

Going nowhere
People in northeastern US states expect snow in winter, but in 2015 few people expected such a severe blizzard.

The climate is the weather patterns a place experiences through the year. Knowledge of climates helps meteorologists to predict what the weather is likely to be several months ahead. However, since global warming has made climates more unpredictable, meteorologists can no longer rely on the past alone to help them predict the future. Meteorologists now study changes in ocean currents and the **jet stream** high in the atmosphere.

OCEAN CURRENTS

Currents in the ocean are like rivers. They carry a stream of water from one place to another, often across the ocean. Some carry cold water, others carry hot water.

If the currents change, the weather does, too. For example, the water on the Asian side of the Pacific Ocean is usually warmer than that on the American side. But every two to seven years, a warm current flows south along the west coast of South America. Meteorologists know that the eastern Pacific will become wetter and droughts in Southeast Asia may occur when this happens.

In the ring

The third president of the United States, Thomas Jefferson (1743–1826), was one of the first Americans to study weather and climate. For 50 years, he kept a diary of the weather in Williamsburg and Monticello in Virginia. He measured rainfall every day and recorded the temperature of the air at dawn (the coldest time) and between 3 pm and 4 pm, the hottest time.

JET STREAMS

Strong winds blow around 9–14 kilometres (6–9 miles) above Earth's surface. These jet streams affect the weather below them. If a jet stream remains stuck in a particular position, the weather below will not change. However, jet streams move about. Meteorologists use computers to predict what will happen to the jet streams, and this helps them to make better long-term weather forecasts.

Saltwater surfers

Ocean currents are vital for many marine animals, such as crocodiles. They "surf" on currents to help them travel through the water.

23

Chapter three: On top of earth-shaking events

Unlike storms, earthquakes, tsunamis and volcanic eruptions seem to occur without warning. However, there are certain changes that indicate that the earth is about to shatter. The most obvious sign is an increase in earth tremors. Scientists measure and monitor these tremors to help them predict natural disasters.

MEASURING EARTH TREMORS

Scientists use **seismometers** to measure the size of earth tremors and to work out where they are coming from. The first seismometer was invented by Chang Hêng, a Chinese philosopher, more than 2,000 years ago. His device could detect tremors up to 640 kilometres (398 miles) away. Today, seismometers are so sensitive they can pick up major tremors on the other side of the world.

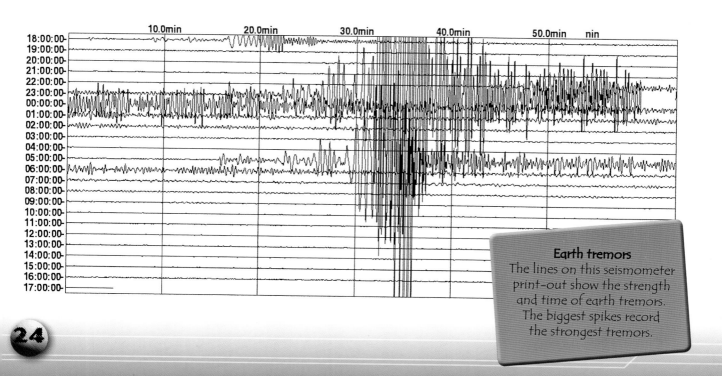

Earth tremors
The lines on this seismometer print-out show the strength and time of earth tremors. The biggest spikes record the strongest tremors.

Breaking through

Scientists have now discovered that a gas called radon escapes through cracks in the rock before an earthquake strikes. Detecting the gas could be the first reliable way of predicting an earthquake. Instruments for detecting radon were once very expensive, but now scientists in Mexico and Europe have invented a much simpler and cheaper device.

CAN ANIMALS PREDICT EARTHQUAKES?

Many people think that animals can sense earthquakes before they happen. They report that dogs, cats and even snakes have behaved oddly before a quake hits. For example, a group of toads abandoned their pond in L'Aquila in Italy a few days before an earthquake hit the city in 2009. Many scientists now think there could be some truth in the claims that reptiles, fish and amphibians behave oddly before an earthquake. They say that rocks under pressure before the quake produce electrically charged particles, which the animals living in water in ponds or in the ground could detect.

Wise toads
Toads can behave oddly before an earthquake. These animals will abandon their ponds if they sense earth tremors beneath them.

Predicting a volcanic eruption

There are three types of volcano – active, dormant and extinct volcanoes. A dormant volcano is one that has not been active for hundreds of years, but scientists are aware that it could erupt again. An extinct volcano is not expected to erupt ever again. Dormant volcanoes are the hardest to predict. They could erupt at any time, but they might not do so for hundreds of years ahead.

Feel the heat
Magma radiates heat. The lighter yellow parts are the hottest, and the darker patches are cooler – but are still incredibly hot.

MONITORING EARTH TREMORS

Most eruptions follow an increase in the size and number of earth tremors. Small earth tremors can occur off and on for months before a volcano erupts, so it is difficult for scientists to use them as an accurate predictor. Nevertheless, seismometers are vital because they provide scientists with data about what is happening in the earth below a volcano.

MONITORING MAGMA AND GASES

The cones of active volcanoes are often filled with hot, bubbling magma. The magma may erupt into a fountain that falls back into the cone. If these small eruptions become more violent, scientists know that a bigger eruption may be brewing. The gases in the magma and those that escape from vents in the volcano give scientists a lot of useful information. First, the amount of gas that escapes usually increases before an eruption and there is often a change in the type of gases released. Second, the amount and type of gases in the magma tell scientists what kind of eruption to expect – either an explosive one or an effusive one.

Winning or losing?

There are more than 1,000 active and dormant volcanoes on Earth. Scientists cannot monitor them all, and it is particularly difficult to monitor volcanoes under the oceans. Instead, scientists monitor the volcanoes that they think are most likely to erupt soon. Even so, they are sometimes taken by surprise. In 1963, a new island formed by a volcano suddenly appeared off the coast of Iceland!

Active volcano
Kilauea Volcano in Hawaii is clearly an active volcano. Gases erupt from both its cone and side vents.

Time to escape

Scientists issue warnings when they think a volcano is going to explode. Warnings can save lives if people are able to quickly escape to safety. Scientists also warn people when they detect an earthquake under the ocean. Tsunamis often follow undersea earthquakes. Those closest to the earthquake may have only minutes to escape, but those further away have longer.

Earthquake drill
Students in Xingtai City in China regularly practise what to do if an earthquake occurs. They know that the drill could save their lives.

TSUNAMI
EVACUATION
ROUTE
เส้นทางหนีคลื่นยักษ์
200 m.

TSUNAMIS

Across the deep ocean, tsunami waves travel at about 765 kilometres per hour (475 mph) but slow down to around 64 kilometres per hour (40 mph) in shallow water. Earth tremors travel faster, so scientists are alerted before the tsunami strikes and have a short time to issue warnings. In Japan and other countries that often get tsunamis, a warning siren sounds in coastal cities and villages.

VOLCANOES

When a volcano explodes, it may create a **pyroclastic flow** or a mudslide. A pyroclastic flow is a blast of hot gas and dust that sweeps down a mountainside, burning everything in its path. A mudslide is a mixture of water and mud.

In the ring

Before Mount St. Helens in Washington state, United States, exploded in 1980, part of the mountainside began to bulge. Scientists knew that a disaster was going to happen, but they did not know when. They monitored the volcano constantly. David Johnston (1949–80) was at an observation post about 10 kilometres (6 miles) from the mountain when the explosion occurred. He managed to radio the Volcano Centre in Vancouver, Washington state, with the message "Vancouver! Vancouver! This is it!" After the explosion, no trace of Johnston was found and he was presumed dead.

Chapter four: Building defences

A good way to fight back against natural disasters is to build strong defences. Today, architects and scientists work together to produce buildings, bridges and other structures that are strong enough to stand up if a natural disaster strikes. Unfortunately, many old buildings or those in poor areas have not been built in this way.

Shaken and destroyed
Buildings in the region of Yunnan, China, collapsed when an earthquake struck in 2013.

BUILDING BETTER

The stronger a building is, the less likely it is to be blown down in a storm or to collapse in an earthquake. Buildings that have solid, strong **foundations** and sturdy walls usually survive better. The foundations are the parts buildings that are sunk into the ground. Generally, the deeper they are the better they will survive. Poor people are often worse hit by a natural disaster because they cannot afford to build strong homes.

THE COST

Constructing stronger buildings costs money. Cutting corners to save money can be disastrous. When an earthquake hit Sichuan Province in China in 2008, many children died as schools collapsed. Other public buildings, such as hospitals and factories, were particularly badly damaged too. This led people to suspect that these buildings had not been properly built.

The United Nations has long argued that it is cheaper for governments to spend money making sure that structures are built well, than to pay for the cost of rebuilding them. While the number of natural disasters tripled between the 1960s and the 1990s, the cost of rebuilding increased nearly 10 times. It would have been cheaper to have built better from the start.

Winning or losing?

Defences often have to be built higher or stronger than originally estimated. When a tsunami struck Japan in 2011, the sea walls were not high enough to hold the waves back. In 2005, when Hurricane Katrina struck in New Orleans, United States, the **levees** built to protect the city collapsed because they had not been maintained.

Flood defences

After Hurricane Katrina struck New Orleans, the levees were built bigger and stronger to hold back future floodwaters.

Quakeproof buildings

More people are killed in an earthquake by a building collapsing than by the earthquake itself. Scientists have studied what happens to a building when it is shaken violently and worked out some ways that people can survive it. They discovered that a building not only needs to be strong but it also needs to be flexible, which means that it can move without breaking.

Safe from quakes
Istanbul's international airport was the largest quakeproof building in the world when it opened in 2009.

WHAT HAPPENS TO BUILDINGS?

When an earthquake strikes, the ground ripples, like the surface of a pond when a stone is thrown into it. The ripples move the building up and down and from side to side. The sideways movement is the most damaging. The higher and heavier the building, the greater the damage. One way of making the building safer is to not build it too high and to use lightweight materials. This stops collapse if an earthquake strikes.

BUILT TO MOVE

Architects have found that buildings that use steel mixed with other materials resist earthquakes more effectively than those built of bricks, concrete and glass. Traditional houses built of wood and stone also withstand earthquakes well. Better still, scientists have devised ways for buildings to soak up the movement during an earthquake to protect the rest of the structure. One method is to "float" the building on a network of **ball-bearings**, springs and padded cylinders. The network allows the foundations to move, but not the rest of the building.

Breaking through

Scientists in Germany have invented special seismic wallpaper. It consists of panels made of glass fibre, which hold up the walls during an earthquake. The panels are stuck to the wall with glue. Tests in an earthquake **simulator** show that walls with the seismic wallpaper receive much less damage than walls that were built without it.

Building high
The ACT building in Japan is 45 floors high. As earthquake-resistance technology improves, taller skyscrapers are being built.

Flood defences

Heavy rain, hurricanes and tsunamis all cause serious flooding. Sea walls and levees are the first line of defence against storm surges and waves, but they need to be built high and strong. In 2013, for example, a storm surge hit the east coast of England, causing waves to break through several sea wall defences. Many flood defences that were adequate in the past will now need to be increased as sea levels rise and storms become worse.

NOT THE BEST PLACES TO BUILD

Rivers flood from time to time, particularly in spring when the winter snow melts or after heavy rain. The flat land on either side of a river is called the flood plain. Traditionally, people avoided building on flood plains, but in some places land is now so scarce that many homes are built close to rivers. One way to deal with this is to build homes on stilts, as people in Asia have done for centuries. In the Netherlands, a modern twist is to build homes that slide up steel stilts whenever the water level rises.

Flood gullies
During the wet season in Hong Kong, heavy rain quickly drains from the streets into these concrete gullies.

KEEPING OUT THE WATER

There is much that ordinary people can do to protect their homes and belongings from floodwater. A heavy seal around the whole door keeps the water out far better than using sandbags. Most homes have electric sockets near the floor, but people who live in flood areas can move electric wiring and sockets higher up the wall. They can replace fitted carpet with floor materials that are not damaged by water and can be easily cleaned.

Winning or losing?

As sea levels rise and storms worsen, more people are living in places that are likely to flood. In Bangladesh, most people live on low-lying land around the delta of the mighty river Ganges. They suffer frequent floods from the river and from storm surges. Around 25 per cent of the country floods regularly and nearly 65 per cent is likely to flood.

Living on water

New floating homes have been built on the waterfront of Almere in the Netherlands. They are safe from flooding.

Protection from wind

Scientists research and test ways of making buildings more able to stand up to the extreme winds of hurricanes and tornadoes. The shape and design of a new building is most important, but the materials also help. Wood and concrete that is **reinforced** with steel are the best materials to build with. Existing buildings can also be strengthened to make them more windproof.

Ripped apart
Parts of the roof and walls of this house were torn off and sucked into the air as a tornado passed over it.

BUILDING NEW HOMES

Square houses are strong, but homes with six or eight sides are even better, because they allow the wind to flow around them. Bungalows are popular in areas such as Florida in the United States, which gets many hurricanes. This is because low buildings are safer than tall ones. Once the roof of the house is blown off, the rest is easily damaged. To avoid this happening, the roof must be firmly fixed to the walls and the whole building must be well anchored to the foundations.

PROTECTING EXISTING HOMES

A simple way to make a house more windproof is to have outside doors that open outwards. This makes it harder for the wind to blow the door in! Windows and garage doors can be protected with steel shutters, which can be closed when a storm is approaching. Building a bank of earth against the lower walls strengthens them and also helps to keep the inside of the house cool during the summer months.

Dome house
This house is built to withstand strong winds. Its many slanted roofs form a dome, which deflects the wind.

In the ring
Panneer Selvam is a wind engineer. He made a model to study what happens to a building when a tornado hits it. Usually, wind flows around the sides of a building as well as up and over the top of it. However, Selvam found that when a tornado hits a building, the wind cannot go around it. Instead, it lifts the building up with a force that is up to 10 times stronger than the force of gravity. His work has helped architects to design windproof buildings.

Chapter five: Working with nature

Natural disasters are the worst events that nature can throw at us, but we can also use nature to prevent the damage they cause or lessen their effects. At the moment, many of the things we do make the impact of natural disasters worse, not better. Scientists say that trees and other plants could be our allies in combating storms, floods and droughts.

HOLDING ONTO SOIL

Tree roots growing on mountainsides and hillsides soak up water and keep the soil in place. In many places, the trees have been cut down to provide wood for building homes and to sell to other countries to earn money. When the trees have gone, water pours straight down the slopes and washes away the soil. This can trigger landslides and mudslides that destroy villages and farmland. By replanting trees, people can prevent this happening. The trees themselves can also provide food, shelter and a source of income.

Bare hillsides
Many trees in this valley have been cut down. This has increased the threat of mudslides occurring in spring, when the winter snow melts and washes away the treeless soil.

PROTECTING COASTS

Mangrove trees grow in the tropics in salty swamps along the coast. Their tangled roots, trunks and branches provide a barrier that slows down tsunamis and storm surges. Southeast Asia was hard hit by the Asian Tsunami in 2004 and has also been affected by several cyclones since. Without the mangrove swamps, the destruction and death toll would have been even worse. Unfortunately, these swamps are often cut down to make room for farmland, shrimp farms and new houses.

Natural protection
Many people are now trying to protect mangrove swamps to preserve the natural protection they provide against the sea.

In the ring

The country of Bangladesh is particularly vulnerable to floods. The rivers flood because melted snow and rain pours into them from the high Himalayan Mountains. Storm surges and rising sea levels cause floods in coastal areas. In 2008, the government of Bangladesh announced that it would plant 100 million trees, mostly along the coast, to protect the area from floods and cyclones.

Battling drought

A drought is a long period without rain. Plants and farm crops that need plenty of water shrivel up and die in a drought. Farmers are used to watering plants in dry periods, using **irrigation** or water from wells. Prolonged droughts are a disaster, however, and can even turn affected areas into desert. As climates change due to global warming, prolonged droughts are becoming far more common.

Oil plant
Rapeseed is grown for animal feed, cooking oil and biofuel. Scientists have produced rapeseed that is more drought resistant.

SHORTAGE OF WATER

It is not only droughts that cause a lack of water. In many countries, farmers and cities have relied on water pumped from rivers and wells below the ground. When more water is taken out than is replaced each year, these supplies begin to dry up. And as droughts increase, there is even less water to replace the water being used.

PLANTS THAT NEED LESS WATER

One way to combat water shortage is to plant vegetables and other crops that do not need much water. They include black-eyed peas, Bambara groundnuts and squash. They even include tomatoes and melons. Rice, wheat and most cereal crops need water, although some, such as rye, use less. Scientists have pointed out that even drought-resistant crops cannot survive a prolonged drought and that they are not a lasting solution.

Breaking through

Scientists in Argentina have experimented with **genes** to make crops more drought resistant. Sunflowers grow well with little water, and scientists have now identified the genes in the sunflower that are responsible. They have taken these genes and added them to the seeds of other plants, such as soya beans, to see what would happen. When the modified seeds grew into plants, the soya beans needed less water and produced up to twice as many beans. The scientists have also tested the genes with wheat and corn.

Dying of thirst
Changing a plant's genes can make crops more drought resistant, but nothing can make plants entirely droughtproof.

The fight continues: Is science winning?

Scientists understand why natural disasters occur. They are able to predict them more accurately, and warn the public, so that people can protect themselves. Scientists have warned that global warming and climate change will make natural disasters more frequent and more damaging. It is up to people, and governments in particular, to heed their warnings and take action now.

Colliding comet?
Natural disasters could strike from space. A comet is one of the many objects that might crash into Earth from space.

CATASTROPHE FROM OUTER SPACE

Meteoroids are lumps of rock travelling through space. Sometimes they are pulled by gravity towards Earth. Most of them are small and burn up as they fall through the atmosphere. We see these objects as streaks of light in the night sky. A large object, however, could cause immense damage.

ASTRONOMIC COLLISIONS

If a very large meteoroid hits the land, it would explode and throw huge amounts of dust into the air. The dust would be so thick it would block out the Sun. Earth would become as cold and dark as an Arctic winter, killing plants and most animals. Scientists think that an explosion like this killed the dinosaurs 65 million years ago. The good news is that scientists say that such a catastrophic collision is extremely rare, but they watch out for them anyway.

Winning or losing?

A meteoroid called Apophis is expected to pass close to Earth in 2029. Could it hit us? In 2004, NASA said that it might, but then changed their minds and said that it would not. Russian scientists disagreed, and predicted it could crash into Earth in 2036. Both teams are monitoring Apophis. If it gets too close, NASA plans to hit it with an unmanned spacecraft to make it change direction.

Meteoroid crater
This huge crater in Arizona was made when a meteoroid crashed into Earth between 20,000 and 50,000 years ago.

The disaster story

65 million years ago
A very large meteoroid crashes into Earth, causing an explosion that is believed to have killed off the dinosaurs and many other species.

AD 79
Mount Vesuvius in Italy explodes, burying both the cities of Herculaneum and Pompeii in volcanic ash. Pliny the Younger witnesses the disaster and later writes the first account of a volcanic eruption.

AD 132
The Chinese philosopher Chang Hêng invents the first seismometer, an instrument that registers earth tremors and indicates the direction that they came from.

1700s
American president Thomas Jefferson keeps a weather diary for 50 years, providing the first detailed accounts of the weather in one place over a long period of time.

1870s
Father Benito Viñes, a priest in Cuba, becomes the first meteorologist to observe storm clouds and use them to predict a hurricane before it arrives.

1970
A cyclone hits the island of Bhola in the delta of the river Ganges, killing between 300,000 and 500,000 people.

1976
An earthquake in Tangshan, China kills between 255,000 and 655,000 people.

1980
Mount St. Helens in Washington state explodes.

2004
The Asian Tsunami hits coasts around the Indian Ocean, killing more than 230,000 people. Lack of an early warning system meant that most people are alerted only when massive waves hit the shore.

2005
Hurricane Katrina causes devastating flooding in New Orleans in the United States.

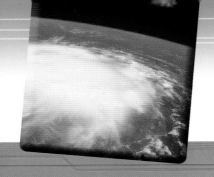

1883
The volcanic island of Krakatoa in Indonesia explodes, killing over 50,000 people. The explosion is heard 4,800 kilometres (2,983 miles) away, on the other side of the Indian Ocean.

1915
Alfred Wegener publishes his theory of continental drift, which says that Earth's crust is divided into large plates that are slowly moving.

1956
The National Hurricane Center in Miami, United States, is formed to monitor hurricanes and issue warnings.

1960
NASA launches *Tiros 1*, the first ever weather satellite. The satellite sends television pictures of the clouds moving across the surface of Earth.

1960
The most powerful earthquake ever recorded hits Valdivia in Chile. It is called the Great Chilean Earthquake, and it triggers a tsunami that affects islands and countries in and around the Pacific Ocean.

2008
A Tsunami Early Warning System for the Indian Ocean goes into operation. Work on it began after the Asian Tsunami in 2004 and was coordinated by the United Nations.

2011
An earthquake 70 kilometres (43 miles) off the north-east coast of Japan creates a tsunami with waves up to 40.5 metres (133 feet) high.

2014
Cyclone Hudhud brings wind speeds of up to 200 kilometres per hour (124 mph) as it passes over the Indian coastline.

2015
In Nepal, southern Asia, at least 8,000 are killed and thousands injured by an earthquake. Many roads are blocked due to landslides caused by the quake.

Glossary

avalanche mass of snow that slides rapidly down a mountain

ball-bearing small metal ball that allows one thing to move easily against another

current flow of liquid, such as water, or gases, such as air

cyclone tropical storm that brings very strong winds and rain

drought unusually long period without rain

earth tremor shaking or trembling of the ground

fertile able to produce crops easily

flexible able to bend or move without snapping or cracking

fossil fuel oil, coal and gas, which are formed from the remains of living plants or animals over millions of years

foundations parts of a building below the ground that support the rest of the building

gene part of a living cell that is passed from parents to offspring

global warming increase in the average temperature on the surface of Earth

hurricane enormous storm of intense wind and rain that begins at sea and then travels inland

irrigation pipes, ditches or sprinklers that supply the land with water taken from elsewhere

jet stream fast-moving current of air higher in the atmosphere than where the weather usually forms

lava hot, runny rock that has erupted out of a volcano

levee high bank along a river or lake to stop water flooding onto the land

magma hot, liquid rock under the surface of Earth

mangrove tree tree that grows in salty water in tropical swamps along the coast

meteoroid piece of metal or rock that is moving through space

meteorologist scientist who studies weather patterns on Earth

monsoon strong wind that blows across southern Asia. In summer it blows from the Indian Ocean over the land, bringing heavy rains.

pyroclastic flow cloud of hot gas, ash and rocks that flows very quickly down the side of a volcano

radar device that bounces radio waves off objects and records their positions on a screen

reinforced made stronger

seismic related to or caused by volcanoes or earthquakes

seismometer instrument that measures and records earth tremors

simulator device that reproduces the conditions of a particular situation or event

storm surge unusual rise in the level of the surface of the ocean due to a hurricane

tornado short-lived but intense storm with extremely powerful winds that usually form below a large thundercloud

tsunami large wave or waves created by an underwater earthquake or volcano eruption

vent opening that lets gases and magma escape from a volcano

Find out more

BOOKS

Extreme Earth (Visual Explorers), Toby Reynolds and Paul Calver
(Franklin Watts, 2015)

Volcano & Earthquake (Eyewitness), Collectif
(Dorling Kindersley, 2014)

Weather (The Science Behind), Darlene R. Stille
(Raintree, 2013)

Weather Watcher (Eyewitness Activity), John Woodward
(Dorling Kindersley, 2015)

WEBSITES

For video clips and information on natural disasters and different
kinds of landscapes around the world, visit:
www.bbc.co.uk/education/topics/zmq7hyc/resources/2

The European Space Agency (ESA) website has information on natural
disasters, including earthquakes, flooding and volcanoes:
www.esa.int/esaKIDSen/Naturaldisasters.html

Go to the Met Office website to find out more about weather and
climate, and to try out some weather experiments:
www.metoffice.gov.uk/learning/weather-for-kids

Index